An Animal

PIGS
AND PIGLETS

By Emilia Hendrix

Gareth Stevens
PUBLISHING

Please visit our website, www.garethstevens.com. For a free color catalog of all our high-quality books, call toll free 1-800-542-2595 or fax 1-877-542-2596.

Cataloging-in-Publication Data

Hendrix, Emilia.
Pigs and piglets / by Emilia Hendrix.
p. cm. — (An animal family)
Includes index.
ISBN 978-1-4824-3783-6 (pbk.)
ISBN 978-1-4824-3784-3 (6-pack)
ISBN 978-1-4824-3785-0 (library binding)
1. Piglets — Juvenile literature. 2. Swine — Juvenile literature. I. Hendrix, Emilia. II. Title.
SF395.5 H46 2016
636.4'07—d23

First Edition

Published in 2016 by
Gareth Stevens Publishing
111 East 14th Street, Suite 349
New York, NY 10003

Copyright © 2016 Gareth Stevens Publishing

Editor: Ryan Nagelhout
Designer: Andrea Davison-Bartolotta

Photo credits: Cover, p. 1 Burry van den Brink/Shutterstock.com; p. 5 qsharkvu/Shutterstock.com; p. 7 tillsonburg/Getty Images; p. 9 Dmitry Shkurin/Chutterstock.com; pp. 11, 24 (nose) Svietlieisha Olena/ Shutterstock.com; p. 13 Matyas Rehak/Shutterstock.com; p. 15 Elecstasy/iStock/Thinkstock; pp. 17, 24 (sow) Helga Chirk/Shutterstock.com; p. 19 Aumsama/Shutterstock.com; pp. 21, 24 (piglets) Conny Sjostrom/ Shutterstock.com; p. 23 (top left) UbjsP/Shutterstock.com; p. 23 (top right) anopdesignstock/iStock/Thinkstock; p. 23 (bottom left) Nenad Milenkovic-Indi/iStock/Thinkstock; p. 23 (bottom right) tracy-williams-photography/ iStock/Thinkstock.

Printed in the United States of America

CPSIA compliance information: Batch #CW16GS: For further information contact Gareth Stevens, New York, New York at 1-800-542-2595.

Contents

Pigs are smart animals!

Many live on farms.

7

They have a great sense of smell.

Their nose helps them find food.

They roll in mud.
This keeps them cool.

Pigs live together. They have their own families!

Mother pigs are called sows.

They keep their babies safe.

Baby pigs are called piglets.

They are very cute!